KAREN WALLICK

Unlock the Benefits of Real Estate Investing

Discover 4 Key Reasons Why Real Estate Investing Has Become One of Today's Top Investment Strategies

This book was professionally typeset on Reedsy.
Find out more at reedsy.com

Contents

1

Introduction

Welcome to "Unlocking the Benefits of Real Estate Investing," your introduction to real estate investing and some of the reasons why it has emerged as one of today's foremost investment strategies. This book is designed for individuals intrigued by the prospect of employing real estate as an investment strategy but who may lack the necessary experience or foundational knowledge to confidently make their first investment purchase. In the pages that follow, we will unlock the same doors that so many investors have already walked through today, making real estate a powerhouse in the world of investments. This book will serve as a set of keys, providing insights into some of the advantages that real estate investing can offer.

The first key opens the door to the benefits of property appreciation. Real estate possesses an unparalleled ability to appreciate over time, rooted in the growth of cities and the ever-changing landscape of communities. Unlike the nature of some investments, real estate stands firm, with each structure a testament to the value that continues to unfold with every passing year.

Our second key opens the door of cash flow generation. Real estate, particularly through rental properties, offers a steady stream of passive income. This is not merely an investment; it is an interplay where money works in the background, creating financial freedom that allows investors to break free from the shackles of the traditional nine-to-five grind.

As we advance, the third key opens the door to a powerful tool called leverage. Leveraging equity transcends the limitations of capital. This strategic use of borrowed capital amplifies returns, enabling control over larger assets with a fraction of the initial investment.

The final key opens the door of tax benefits. Real estate becomes not just an investment but a sanctuary for those seeking strategic fiscal advantages. It offers tax benefits like deductions, depreciation, 1031 exchanges, and many others, aligning with the financial goals of savvy investors.

It's time to take your first step into the world of mystery that will soon become a sanctuary of financial independence. As we turn the pages ahead, keep these four keys in mind: property appreciation, generating cash flow, leveraging equity, and tax benefits. Each key unlocks a unique facet of real estate's transformative potential, propelling individuals into a world where financial success is not just an aspiration but an achievable reality.

2

Property Appreciation

I n the world of real estate, one shocking fact echoes through financial history: the staggering appreciation of property. Property appreciation refers to the increase in the value of a real estate asset over time. Picture this: there are instances where a property purchased for a modest sum decades ago has transformed into an asset of exponential value. Property appreciation is a primary consideration for real estate investors and homeowners, as it directly impacts the potential return on investment and equity accumulation. Let's explore how gaining insights into the drivers of property appreciation, strategic property selection, and maximizing the potential for property value growth becomes the first foundational key to unlocking financial success.

Understanding Property Appreciation

Property appreciation is not solely subject to market whims; rather, it's a dynamic force shaped by a multitude of influential factors. Understanding economic growth, neighborhood development, improvements in infrastructure, and shifting demographics provides investors with a reliable compass to navigate the nature of real estate markets. By recognizing how these factors intersect, investors can make informed decisions, identifying opportunities for growth and potential risks.

Economic growth serves as a catalyst for property appreciation. As economies expand, job opportunities increase, driving population growth and enhancing the overall desirability of a region. This surge in demand for housing, both residential and commercial, exerts upward pressure on property values. Businesses can flourish in economically vibrant areas, leading to heightened demand for commercial spaces and contributing to the appreciation of commercial real estate. Additionally, robust economic growth often prompts infrastructure development and urban renewal projects, further enhancing the attractiveness of a locality.

Neighborhood development plays a pivotal role in influencing property appreciation by shaping the overall character and appeal of an area. When neighborhoods undergo thoughtful and strategic development, including improvements in infrastructure, amenities, and community spaces, the perceived value of properties within that vicinity tends to rise. Aesthetically pleasing landscapes, enhanced security measures, and the establishment of cultural or recreational facilities contribute to the desirability of the neighborhood, attracting prospective buyers or tenants.

Improvements in infrastructure exert a significant influence on property appreciation, enhancing the overall desirability and value of real estate. Upgraded infrastructure, such as the development of new roads, public transportation systems, and utility enhancements, not only improves accessibility but also contributes to convenience and quality of life. As transportation becomes more efficient and connectivity improves, the accessibility of neighborhoods to commercial centers, amenities, and employment hubs increases, making properties within proximity more attractive to potential buyers and tenants. Additionally, enhanced infrastructure often signals economic growth and urban development, fostering a positive perception of the neighborhood and prompting increased demand for real estate. Consequently, properties located in areas with improved infrastructure are poised to experience higher appreciation rates as they become integral parts of well-connected and thriving communities.

Shifting demographics exert a profound influence on property appreciation as evolving population dynamics redefine preferences and demands in the real estate market. Changes in demographics, such as the influx of young professionals, retirees, or diverse cultural communities, directly impact the types of properties in demand. Understanding these demographic shifts allows investors to anticipate trends and tailor their real estate portfolios accordingly. For instance, a growing urban population might drive demand for centrally located, high-density housing, while an aging demographic may elevate the appeal of retirement communities or properties with accessible amenities.

This holistic comprehension serves as a strategic advantage, enabling investors to adapt to market dynamics and position themselves for success in the ever-evolving realm of real estate. For further insights on these factors and their impact on property values, investors can turn to reputable real estate market reports, economic analyses, and demographic studies available from sources such as government agencies like U.S. Census Bureau and HUD, real estate research firms like Zillow and CoreLogic, and academic databases like JSTOR and Google Scholar.

Strategic Property Selection

The expression "location, location, location" has never more true than in the pursuit of property appreciation. Strategic property selection involves not only choosing properties wisely but also identifying emerging neighborhoods before they reach their prime. Savvy investors have an eye for potential; they understand that buying into a neighborhood on the cusp of transformation can yield exponential returns.

Timing is the key in this process. Investing when an area is in the beginning stages of growth can position investors to ride the wave of appreciation as the community blossoms. It's about seeing the potential before it becomes mainstream knowledge. This strategy requires a keen understanding of market trends, economic indicators, and a foresight that sets successful investors apart.

Maximizing Appreciation

To truly harness the power of appreciation, investors must go beyond passive ownership. Maximizing appreciation involves active strategies that enhance the value of the property over time. This could include renovations, strategic improvements, and adapting to evolving market demands.

To illustrate these concepts, let's dive into maximizing appreciation through hypothetical scenarios. These examples will showcase how astute investors can transform properties, not just as shelters but as dynamic assets in their portfolios.

Scenario 1: Suburban Oasis – The Green Transformation

Nestled in the heart of a growing suburban community, a dilapidated property became the canvas for an investor's vision, showcasing how residential real estate could be transformed into an idyllic haven while maximizing appreciation.

The property, initially overlooked due to its dated exterior and neglected landscaping, caught the eye of a savvy investor with a penchant for green living. Recognizing the increasing demand for sustainable, eco-friendly homes, the investor embarked on a comprehensive renovation. The transformation included energy-efficient upgrades, solar panels, and a lush, water-saving landscape that not only elevated the property's aesthetics but also positioned it as a model of sustainable living.

As the residence evolved into a green oasis, it attracted a wave of environmentally conscious buyers. The strategic decision to invest in sustainable features not only aligned with contemporary lifestyle preferences but also significantly enhanced the property's market value. The ripple effect extended beyond the individual property, influencing neighboring homes to adopt similar eco-friendly practices.

This scenario exemplifies how a strategic focus on modern trends and sustainability can maximize appreciation in residential real estate. The investor not only revitalized a property but cultivated a market niche, turning a dated residence into a dynamic asset that reflected the values of a new generation of homeowners.

Scenario 2: Historic Charm – The Restoration Renaissance

In a historic neighborhood with rows of aging brownstones, an investor saw not just neglected structures but a canvas for restoring and maximizing appreciation through the artful preservation of architectural charm.

This scenario unfolds in an area known for its rich history, where a collection of Victorian-era brownstones had fallen into disrepair. The investor recognized the inherent value in preserving the unique architectural features of these homes while introducing modern amenities to meet contemporary expectations. The restoration process involved meticulous attention to detail, from restoring ornate moldings to reviving original hardwood floors.

The restored brownstones became an embodiment of timeless elegance, attracting a discerning clientele appreciative of historical aesthetics coupled with modern comforts. The investor's commitment to preserving the neighborhood's historical integrity had a cascading effect on property values, as the entire area experienced a resurgence of interest and investment.

This scenario highlights the transformative potential of maximizing appreciation in residential real estate through historic restoration. By recognizing the value of the neighborhood's architectural heritage and infusing it with contemporary comforts, the investor not only elevated individual properties but contributed to the revitalization of an entire community.

In the next chapter, we'll unravel the fundamentals of Generating Cash Flow through rental income. Together, Property Appreciation and Cash Flow form the backbone of a successful real estate investment strategy, creating wealth that stands the test of time.

3

Cash Flow Generation

I n real estate investing, consistent cash flow is crucial for long-term success. This chapter explores the basics of cash flow, strategies for optimizing it through property management, and the resilience needed during economic downturns.

Basics of Cash Flow

Cash flow is the heartbeat of residential real estate investing. At its essence, cash flow is the net income generated by a property after deducting all operating expenses and mortgage payments. Understanding the Basics of Cash Flow is foundational to navigating the intricate landscape of real estate investments.

Income Sources:

Although there are many different investment strategies that can be used to generate income through real estate, the primary source of income in residential real estate is rental payments from tenants. This revenue stream is the lifeblood of cash flow, providing a consistent infusion of funds. It is crucial to set rental rates that strike a balance between market demands and profitability. Additionally, other income sources may include fees for services provided, such as parking spaces, laundry facilities, or pet deposits.

Operating Expenses:

To determine the viability of cash flow, it's imperative to comprehend and factor in operating expenses. These encompass a spectrum of costs, including property management fees, property taxes, insurance premiums, maintenance, utilities, and potential homeowner association (HOA) fees. The key is to anticipate and accurately estimate these expenditures to avoid unpleasant surprises that can erode cash flow.

Mortgage Payments:

Another aspect of the cash flow equation is mortgage payments. Investors must factor in the principal and interest portions of their mortgage obligations. The terms of the mortgage, including interest rates and the loan duration, significantly influence the cash flow dynamics. A positive cash flow occurs when the income generated exceeds these mortgage payments.

Positive Cash Flow:

A positive cash flow is the golden objective for real estate investors. It signifies that the property is generating surplus income after covering all expenses and mortgage obligations. This surplus not only provides financial stability but also offers the flexibility to reinvest in the property or expand the investment portfolio.

Practical tools, such as a cash flow calculator, serve as a valuable resource for real estate investors to analyze and optimize the financial performance of their residential rental properties. To Find and utilize a cash flow calculator for residential rental properties, start by searching for reputable online tools or software specifically designed for real estate investors. Many websites and platforms offer free or subscription-based calculators tailored to assess cash flow. Remember to read user reviews, and if available, opt for tools that offer trial periods or free versions. This allows you to test the calculator's features and functionality before committing to a subscription. Once you've found a suitable calculator, input key financial details such as rental income, operating expenses (including property management fees, taxes, insurance, maintenance, and utilities), and mortgage details (loan amount, interest rate, and duration). The calculator will process this information to provide a clear breakdown of the property's potential cash flow. Regularly updating the figures as market conditions or expenses change allows investors to make informed decisions about property acquisitions or adjustments to rental rates.

Optimizing Cash Flow through Strategic Property Management

In real estate investing, effective property management is crucial for optimizing cash flow. It goes beyond basic maintenance, involving strategic coordination to maximize income and minimize expenses.

Thorough Tenant Screening:

A crucial aspect of successful property management involves implementing a thorough tenant screening process to foster a secure and stable rental environment. Utilizing various resources can significantly enhance the effectiveness of this screening process. Conducting comprehensive background checks is essential, and online services like TransUnion, Experian, or Equifax can provide detailed information about a prospective tenant's rental history, criminal record, and eviction history. Additionally, credit evaluations play a pivotal role in assessing a tenant's financial stability. Platforms such as Credit Karma or AnnualCreditReport.com allow property managers to obtain credit reports and scores, aiding in the evaluation of a tenant's ability to meet financial obligations. Seeking references from previous landlords is another valuable strategy, offering insights into a tenant's past rental behavior and reliability. Employing a combination of these resources not only strengthens the tenant screening process but also contributes to the overall financial health of the property by securing reliable and responsible long-term tenants.

Cost-Effective Maintenance Measures:

Property maintenance is inevitable, but the key is to approach it with a strategic mindset. To implement cost-effective maintenance measures, property managers can leverage various resources and techniques. Regular inspections conducted by the property management team or hired professionals help identify potential issues early on, allowing for timely intervention and minimizing the overall repair costs. Proactive repairs, based on the findings of these inspections, can address minor issues before they escalate into more significant problems. Utilizing online platforms like HomeAdvisor or Angie's List can assist in finding reliable and reasonably priced local contractors for specific maintenance tasks. Additionally, embracing preventive maintenance schedules and adopting DIY solutions for minor repairs can further cut down on expenses. By combining these resources and strategies, property managers can not only preserve the property's value but also safeguard the cash flow by minimizing unexpected and costly repairs while ensuring the property remains attractive to tenants.

Market-Driven Rental Rates:

To optimize cash flow, it is crucial for property managers to grasp the dynamics of the local rental market. Conducting routine market analyses is key, and various resources can assist in obtaining the necessary information. Online platforms such as Zillow, Rentometer, or local real estate websites offer insights into current rental trends, helping property managers align their rates with market standards. Accessing data on comparable properties in the vicinity can aid in determining the fair market value of a rental unit. This strategic approach allows property managers to set competitive rental rates that accurately reflect the property's value and amenities. By leveraging these resources, managers can position their properties effectively in the market, attracting tenants while maximizing income potential.

Streamlined Operations:

Efficient property management requires the optimization of operations to reduce unnecessary expenses. Leveraging technology is instrumental in achieving streamlined communication, efficient financial tracking, and effective property maintenance. Reputable tools and property management software play a vital role in this process. Platforms such as Buildium, AppFolio, or Rent Manager offer comprehensive solutions for property managers. These digital tools not only simplify administrative tasks but also provide real-time insights into income and expenses. By utilizing these resources, property managers can enhance their operational efficiency, ensuring a seamless management process and empowering investors with the information needed to make well-informed decisions.

Proactive Communication:

Open and proactive communication with tenants is another facet of effective property management. Establishing clear lines of communication fosters positive tenant relationships, reducing turnover rates and vacancy periods. A tenant who feels valued is more likely to stay longer, providing a stable income source and reducing the costs associated with finding new tenants.

Lease Structure and Renewals:

Thoughtful structuring of leases and effective management of renewals play a pivotal role in influencing cash flow for rental properties. Ensuring the stability of cash flow can be achieved by carefully crafting long-term leases with gradual rent increases, providing both landlords and tenants with predictability. To gain guidance on structuring leases and managing renewals, landlords can turn to legal resources, consult with real estate professionals, or explore reputable websites offering templates and advice on lease agreements. Strategic renewal planning is equally essential to prevent gaps in rental income. Landlords may consider offering incentives for lease renewals, such as maintenance upgrades or rent discounts, to foster tenant loyalty and encourage them to extend their lease agreements. By seeking guidance on lease structuring and renewal strategies, property owners can navigate these processes more effectively, contributing to the overall financial health of their investment.

Risk Mitigation:

Successful property management necessitates the implementation of risk mitigation strategies, encompassing various tasks. To ensure adequate insurance coverage, property owners can consult with insurance agents for personalized advice or explore comparison websites such as Policygenius and Insure.com to find the most suitable plans. Conducting regular property inspections to identify potential issues can be facilitated through local inspection services, mobile apps like HappyCo, or professional inspection firms. Staying informed about legal regulations and obligations is crucial, and property managers can access legal resources like Nolo or Rocket Lawyer, attend seminars offered by local real estate associations, or explore online platforms such as LegalZoom for comprehensive guidance. By proactively addressing risks through these diverse resources, property managers can minimize the likelihood of unexpected financial setbacks that might otherwise impact the property's cash flow.

Navigating Economic Downturns

The resilience of cash flow truly shines during economic downturns, a reality recognized by two compelling case studies that illuminate successful cash flow management strategies when faced with economic challenges.

Case Study 1: The 2008 Financial Crisis and Rental Resilience

In the crucible of the 2008 financial crisis, one astute investor navigated the storm by recalibrating their strategy towards the rental market. Recognizing the prevailing economic upheaval and the diminishing allure of homeownership, the investor made a strategic decision to shift from selling properties, a challenging endeavor in a depreciating market, to emphasizing rental offerings.

This pivot was not just a reactive measure; it was a proactive stance that aligned with the changing landscape. The demand for rental housing surged as economic uncertainties prompted many to reconsider long-term commitments associated with homeownership. By redirecting focus towards rental properties, the investor not only shielded themselves from the market's downward spiral but positioned their portfolio to capitalize on a burgeoning rental market.

This adaptive strategy not only preserved cash flow during a turbulent period but also laid the foundation for substantial gains in the future. As the market eventually rebounded, the investor found themself in a prime position with a portfolio of income-generating rental properties. The resilience demonstrated during the crisis underscored the importance of strategic decision-making and the symbiotic relationship between adaptive cash flow management and long-term investment success.

Case Study 2: The COVID-19 Pandemic and Adaptive Strategies

In the wake of the unprecedented challenges posed by the COVID-19 pandemic, another investor faced the potential disruption of income within their portfolio of rental properties. With lockdowns, economic uncertainties, and changing tenant dynamics, the landscape demanded agility and foresight.

Instead of succumbing to the potential downturn, this investor embraced adaptive strategies to safeguard and sustain cash flow. Flexible leasing terms were introduced to accommodate the evolving needs and financial constraints of tenants facing unprecedented circumstances. Proactive communication with tenants became paramount, fostering trust and solidarity during a period of uncertainty.

Technology became a key ally in remote property management. Leveraging digital platforms, the investor streamlined operations, enabling efficient communication, rent collection, and property maintenance without the need for physical proximity. This not only ensured the continuity of income but also positioned the portfolio for continued success post-pandemic.

By prioritizing tenant retention and embracing technological solutions, this investor not only weathered the storm but emerged with a resilient portfolio ready to capitalize on the recovering market. The adaptive strategies deployed during the pandemic became a testament to the importance of flexibility, innovation, and tenant-centric approaches in maintaining and enhancing cash flow resilience.

In both case studies, the common thread is the ability of investors to adapt their strategies in response to external shocks. The symbiosis between strategic shifts, resilient cash flow management, and long-term success is evident. However, the narrative extends beyond the steady rhythm of cash flow. Real estate investing is enhanced by the symbiotic relationship between cash flow and leveraging equity. Positive cash flow establishes a robust base for investments and serves as a tool to amplify financial capabilities. Leveraging equity enables investors to strategically harness the potential of borrowed capital, significantly magnifying the effects of their initial investments.

4

Leveraging Equity

I s there a practical value in the equity we accumulate in these properties that can lead to lasting prosperity? In exploring the concept of leveraging equity, we aim to demystify this question and reveal the transformative opportunities that arise with equity built from real estate.

Borrowing Against Equity

Equity, often characterized as the silent partner in your real estate investments, represents the difference between the property's market value and the outstanding mortgage balance. While it sits on your balance sheet, its full potential remains dormant until activated through leveraging. This financial maneuver is akin to unlocking a treasure chest, breathing vitality into equity and turning it into an active force within your investment portfolio.

Leveraging equity is a practical use of borrowed capital. Borrowed capital, when employed judiciously, amplifies your ability to generate returns on investment. This amplification effect goes beyond the nominal value of the borrowed funds; it is about strategically leveraging these funds to acquire additional assets, diversify your portfolio, or enhance the value of existing properties.

Strategies for Leveraging Success

Leveraging equity involves practical considerations rather than just theoretical appeal. We'll explore tools like home equity loans, cash-out refinancing, and even seller financing, assessing each for its potential in investment scenarios.

Home Equity Loans: Tapping into Built-Up Equity

Fundamentals:

A Home Equity Loan, also known as a second mortgage, allows homeowners to tap into the equity they have built up in their property. The loan is secured by the home itself, utilizing the property as collateral. Homeowners receive a lump sum upfront, often with a fixed interest rate, and repay the loan over a set period. This strategy is particularly advantageous for those looking to fund specific projects, such as home renovations by leveraging the accrued value in their property.

How it Works:

Consider a scenario where you own a property with a market value higher than your outstanding mortgage. The equity in your home represents the difference. A Home Equity Loan allows you to borrow against this equity, providing a lump sum that you can then use strategically. The interest on home equity loans is often tax-deductible, adding a layer of financial benefit for eligible borrowers.

Key Considerations:

While Home Equity Loans offer liquidity and tax advantages, they come with a responsibility to meet monthly payments. Defaulting on these payments could jeopardize your home, as it serves as collateral. Therefore, careful consideration of your ability to repay and the purpose of the borrowed funds is crucial in leveraging this strategy effectively.

Cash-Out Refinancing: Restructuring for Financial Growth

Fundamentals:

Cash-Out Refinancing involves restructuring your existing mortgage, replacing it with a new one that exceeds the current loan balance. The excess amount is paid out to the homeowner in cash, providing a lump sum that can be used for various purposes. This strategy is particularly enticing when interest rates are favorable or when the property has appreciated, offering an opportunity to access a larger sum while maintaining a single mortgage payment.

How it Works:

Suppose you own a property with a mortgage, and its value has increased over time. With Cash-Out Refinancing, you would refinance your current mortgage for an amount higher than what you owe. The difference between the new loan and the existing mortgage is paid out to you in cash. This lump sum can be employed for strategic investments, such as acquiring additional properties or funding substantial renovations.

Key Considerations:

While Cash-Out Refinancing provides immediate access to funds and the potential for lower interest rates, it extends the repayment period. This means that, over time, you may pay more interest. Therefore, careful evaluation of the long-term financial implications and your ability to manage the extended mortgage is crucial before opting for this leveraging strategy.

Seller Finance

Seller financing can also serve as a leveraging tool in real estate transactions, offering an alternative method for buyers to secure funding while providing sellers with increased flexibility. The fundamental concept involves the property seller acting as the lender, facilitating the purchase by extending credit directly to the buyer. This approach can be advantageous for both parties, and it functions as a leveraging tool in the following ways:

1. Access to Properties with Limited Financing Options:

Seller financing allows buyers to access properties that may be challenging to finance through traditional lenders. This is particularly beneficial for individuals with limited credit history or unconventional financial situations.

2. Flexible Terms:

Unlike conventional mortgages, seller financing permits more flexibility in negotiating terms. Buyers and sellers can tailor the agreement to their specific needs, determining the interest rate, repayment schedule, and down payment based on mutual agreement.

3. Opportunity for Higher Sales Price:

Sellers can potentially secure a higher sales price by offering financing. This can be an attractive incentive for buyers who may be willing to pay a premium in exchange for more favorable financing terms.

4. Increased Liquidity for Sellers:

By acting as the lender, sellers receive regular payments over time, potentially providing a steady income stream. This liquidity can be beneficial for sellers looking to reinvest in other opportunities or diversify their financial portfolio.

5. Mitigation of Market Challenges:

In a market where conventional financing may be difficult to obtain, seller financing can serve as a strategic tool for both buyers and sellers. It enables transactions to proceed in situations where traditional lending institutions might be more cautious.

In summary, seller financing acts as a leveraging tool by providing an alternative financing avenue for real estate transactions. It allows buyers to access properties and secure funding that may not be readily available through traditional channels, while offering sellers increased flexibility, potential for higher returns, and the opportunity to leverage the proceeds for further real estate investments.

Now that you've learned a few ways to leverage equity as a practical tool to enhance the impact of your initial investments, we journey on to the next chapter on tax benefits. We acknowledge the synergistic relationship between leveraging equity and tax advantages, which contributes to more effective wealth creation.

5

Tax Benefits

I nvesting in real estate isn't just about acquiring properties and collecting cash—it's a strategic financial move uniquely positioned to harness a multitude of tax benefits. The allure lies not only in the bricks and mortar but in the advantageous landscape of the tax code. In this chapter, we delve into some of the distinctive tax benefits that real estate investors enjoy, uncovering the intricacies of deductions, the power of depreciation, the technical 1031 exchange, and the strategic legal structures that amplify financial advantages.

Deductions and Write-Offs:

Real estate investors have access to a valuable array of deductions and write-offs, establishing a strong foundation for optimizing financial efficiency. Key deductions, such as those for mortgage interest and property taxes, offer immediate relief by reducing taxable income. To identify other deductible items, investors can leverage resources like real estate tax guides, accounting professionals, and online platforms such as the IRS website, which provides comprehensive information on allowable deductions. These additional deductions encompass various operating expenses, from insurance premiums to maintenance costs and utility bills. Exploring reliable resources ensures investors are well-informed about the diverse deductions available within the tax code.

Depreciation: The Silent Wealth Builder

Depreciation is a tax-recognized acknowledgment of the gradual decline in the value of a property over time. This allowance enables investors to allocate a portion of the property's value as an expense. It works by assigning a specific lifespan to different components of the property, such as the building structure or appliances, based on established guidelines by tax authorities. Unlike traditional expenses, depreciation is a non-cash deduction, emphasizing the inevitable aging of the property with substantial financial significance.

Investors can annually deduct a portion of the property's value over its designated useful life, spreading this expense over several years. The calculation of depreciation involves factors like the property's cost, its estimated useful life, and the chosen depreciation method, commonly either straight-line or accelerated. This extended deduction goes beyond immediate expenses, contributing to the property owner's financial efficiency by reducing taxable income over time. As the property ages, this non-cash deduction becomes increasingly valuable, forming a crucial aspect of real estate investment strategies.

More information on property depreciation as a tax benefit can be found from various reputable sources, such as the official IRS website, real estate tax guides, tax professionals, and educational courses. Always ensure that the information you gather is up-to-date and aligns with current tax laws and regulations. Tax codes can undergo changes, so staying informed with recent resources is essential for accurate and effective tax planning.

1031 Tax Exchange

A 1031 tax exchange, named after Section 1031 of the Internal Revenue Code, empowers real estate investors to defer capital gains taxes when selling one property and acquiring another of like-kind. This powerful tool stimulates investment growth by enabling individuals to reinvest proceeds without immediate tax consequences. To dive deeper into the intricacies of 1031 exchanges, investors can turn to authoritative resources such as publications by the IRS, including IRS Publication 544, "Sales and Other Dispositions of Assets," which provides detailed guidelines on like-kind exchanges.

The process involves identifying a replacement property within 45 days of selling the relinquished property and completing the exchange within 180 days. Eligible properties must be of similar nature, broadening options from residential to commercial real estate. For a seamless 1031 exchange experience, investors often seek guidance from qualified intermediaries, who act as facilitators throughout the process. Organizations like the Federation of Exchange Accommodators (FEA) can provide a directory of qualified intermediaries, ensuring compliance with the stringent rules and deadlines associated with 1031 exchanges.

While 1031 exchanges offer substantial tax advantages, staying informed about potential changes or limitations to this provision is crucial. Investors can monitor legislative discussions and updates on tax regulations through official government websites, tax-focused news outlets, and real estate investment forums. Resources like the National Association of Realtors (NAR) and tax advisory websites also offer insights into the latest developments related to 1031 exchanges.

Legal Structures for Tax Optimization: Building a Fortified Framework

In real estate investing, maximizing tax benefits extends beyond individual deductions and depreciation to encompass the strategic domain of legal structures. Real estate investors can optimize tax benefits by choosing legal entities such as Limited Liability Companies (LLCs), S Corporations, or partnerships. The selection of an entity significantly influences tax obligations, with each structure providing distinct advantages, from pass-through taxation to liability protection.

For pass-through taxation and personal liability protection, an LLC stands out. Profits and losses flow directly to individual owners, ensuring income from real estate investments is taxed at favorable rates while safeguarding personal assets.

S Corporations, combining pass-through taxation with a formal corporate structure, offer unique benefits. Investors may reduce self-employment tax liabilities, making S Corporations attractive for those aiming to optimize tax obligations. Navigating the interplay between profit distribution and salary payments becomes a strategic process for minimizing tax liabilities without compromising financial efficiency.

Partnerships, whether general or limited, provide flexibility and simplicity in the tax optimization landscape. Investors can pool resources, share profits, and strategically allocate income and losses. This flexibility allows partners to align with diverse financial goals within the partnership.

To delve deeper into the legal landscape, real estate investors can refer to resources such as publications by the IRS, legal advisors, and real estate investment forums. The IRS website offers valuable information on legal structures and tax considerations for different entities. Legal professionals specializing in real estate taxation can provide personalized guidance, and forums like BiggerPockets allow investors to share insights and experiences.

Understanding the legal framework is crucial for investors aiming to create a robust foundation that maximizes tax benefits and safeguards financial interests. By navigating this legal landscape strategically, investors become architects of their financial destiny, crafting a framework where tax benefits are intricately woven into the foundation of their real estate portfolios.

6

Conclusion

R eal estate stands out as a premier investment avenue for various compelling reasons. Within the pages of this book, you've been introduced to four pivotal factors that justify the prominence of real estate in contemporary investment strategies. From the profound impact of property appreciation to the imperative of generating consistent cash flow, leveraging equity for expansion, and harnessing the unique tax benefits of real estate, each chapter has illuminated a facet of this dynamic and transformative investment approach.

I hope you enjoyed the journey of unlocking not only the key benefits, but a basic infrastructure for success. As you step into the world of real estate investing, may your ventures be as prosperous as the knowledge gained within these pages. The keys to success in real estate are now in your hands; it's up to you to unlock the doors to a future of financial prosperity.

If you discovered valuable insights by reading this book, I would sincerely appreciate it if you could take a moment to share your thoughts by leaving a positive review on Amazon. Your feedback is immensely important to me. Don't forget to keep an eye out for future book releases! While this book was a very basic introduction into the world of real estate investing, I will continue to build onto this knowledge base by opening the doors of the various real estate investment strategies that so many investors have used to build generational wealth and prosperity. Thank you!

7

Resources

The information in this book has been curated through a comprehensive process, integrating thorough online market research with my firsthand experience as a licensed Realtor who is actively engaged in the investment industry.

Research reports. (2012, January 13). www.nar.realtor. https://www.nar.realtor/research-and-statistics/research-reports

Housing and Economic Research. (n.d.). Freddie Mac. https://www.freddiemac.com/research

Kustka, M. (2023, March 7). How Green Building is Transforming the Real Estate Industry | AlphaSense. AlphaSense. https://www.alpha-sense.com/blog/trends/green-building-transforming-real-estate/

Parker, T. (2023, May 16). Cash-Out Refinance vs. Home Equity Loan: What's the Difference? Investopedia. https://www.investopedia.com/mortgage/heloc/refinancing-vs-home-equity-loan/

Tips on rental real estate income, deductions and recordkeeping | Internal Revenue Service. (n.d.). https://www.irs.gov/businesses/small-businesses-self-employed/tips-on-rental-real-estate-income-deductions-and-recordkeeping

Publication 946 (2022), How to Depreciate Property | Internal Revenue Service. (n.d.). https://www.irs.gov/publications/p946

Like-Kind Exchanges - Real estate tax tips | Internal Revenue Service. (n.d.). https://www.irs.gov/businesses/small-businesses-self-employed/like-kind-exchanges-real-estate-tax-tips

About publication 544, Sales and other dispositions of assets | Internal Revenue Service. (n.d.). https://www.irs.gov/forms-pubs/about-publication-544

Choose a business structure. (n.d.). U.S. Small Business Administration. https://www.sba.gov/business-guide/launch-your-business/choose-business-structure

www.ingramcontent.com/pod-product-compliance
Lightning Source LLC
Chambersburg PA
CBHW070848310526
45796CB00014B/284